WARNING

This book is presented only as a means of preserving a unique aspect of the heritage of the martial arts. Neither Ohara Publications nor the author makes any representation, warranty or guarantee that the techniques described or illustrated in this book will be safe or effective in any self-defense situation or otherwise. You may be injured if you apply or train in the techniques of self-defense illustrated in this book, and neither Ohara Publications nor the author is responsible for any such injury that may result. It is essential that you consult a physician regarding whether or not to attempt any technique described in this book. Specific self-defense responses illustrated in this book may not be justified in any particular situation in view of all of the circumstances or under the applicable federal, state or local law. Neither Ohara Publications nor the author makes any representation or warranty regarding the legality or appropriateness of any technique mentioned in this book.

CHI POWER

by William Cheung

Editor: Mike Lee
Art Director: Sergio Onaga

Printed in the United States of America
Library of Congress Catalog Card Number: 86-63060
ISBN 0-89750-110-1

Twentieth printing 2005

BLACK BELT BOOKS
A Division of **OHARA 🔲 PUBLICATIONS, INC.**
World Leader in Martial Arts Publications

Dedication
This book is dedicated to Trudi Martin.

Acknowledgement
Many thanks to the very talented wing chun practitioner Ken Teichmann
for helping me demonstrate some of the techniques in this book.

About the Author

At the age of ten, William Cheung started his training in wing chun kung fu under Yip Man. He was 14 when he decided to follow wing chun as a way of life. He trained full-time under Yip Man's roof, and for the next four years, wing chun took up all of his time. Between 1957 and 1958 Cheung won the kung fu elimination contests in Hong Kong, defeating opponents with many more years experience. During that period, he helped to teach Bruce Lee many of the techniques that Lee would later use in his very successful film career.

From 1959 when he arrived in Australia to pursue his academic studies, Cheung organized small informal groups interested in martial arts. However,

the death of his master, Yip Man, in 1973 marked a turning point in his life. He decided that the traditional taboo placed on the teaching of wing chun to non-Chinese was an anachronistic and unjustifiable xenophobia. Accordingly, he formed the first wing chun kung fu school in Australia in which the full extent of this Chinese art was taught to Australians of both Chinese and Anglo Saxon extraction.

Cheung was appointed as a Chief Instructor to the U.S. Seventh Fleet based in Yukosuka, Japan, and served in that capacity from 1978 to 1980. During this time, he was in charge of the intensive program of close quarter combat for the marines.

Many of Cheung's students have achieved internationa
their martial arts prowess. In 1982 his students won both the
middleweight divisions in the World Invitation Kung Fu Cha
in Hong Kong. Further, Cheung was himself awarded th
BELT Hall of Fame Award as Kung Fu Artist of the Year

In 1984 William Cheung set the world speed punching rec
es per second at Harvard University in Boston. More recently
tively engaged in research and development to improve tra
ecution of techniques, and has been the first in his field to app

mechanical methods such as high speed filming and computer technology in an attempt to empirically analyze the movements of the art of wing chun kung fu. To promulgate his ideas and stimulate and enliven the art, Cheung has authored *Kung Fu Butterfly Swords* and *Kung Fu Dragon Pole* for Ohara.

In recent years, Cheung has been extensively involved in conducting workshop seminars for various groups in different countries around the world including the U.S., England, Germany, France, Italy, Yugoslavia, Belgium, Switzerland, Finland, Canada, New Zealand, and throughout Asia.

Philosophy of Wing Chun

- One who excels as a warrior does not appear formidable;
- One who excels in fighting is never aroused in anger;
- One who excels in defeating his enemy does not join issues;
- One who excels in employing others humbles himself before them.
- This is the virtue of non-contention and matching the sublimity of heaven.

The aim of wing chun kung fu is to develop physical, mental and spiritual awareness. These elements transcend to a higher level of life. Self-awareness, self-respect and a duty to serve should be the goal of every martial artist. The practitioner should meditate on these principles and make peace through the study of kung fu—a way of life.

Origins of the Chi Exercises

The word *chi* in Chinese can mean different things. In the direct translation, it can mean "air" or "breathing." However, when it is taken further, it can mean "energy," "temper," "tension," or "endurance."

China was the first country in the world to develop breathing exercises. The earliest breathing exercise is called *yick kan ging.* This exercise was developed over 5,000 years ago by a Taoist priest named Kwong Shing Sze. It was based on the objective rules of nature with the ultimate aims of preventing and healing disease to achieve longevity.

According to the official record, Kwong Shing Sze passed the original exercises to his follower, Hin Tan Hwang, who handed them down in his family

generation after generation. During the Chow Dynasty, a learned courtier, Li Yee, took them further. It was reported that Li went west out of San Ku Kwan to preach to the Huns. There he met the Buddha, and on a snow mountain in India, taught him the exercises. This was the first time the Chinese ways of breathing and physical exercise reached a foreign country.

In the Han Dynasty, culture and civilization reached a peak. During that time, the most prominent account of this knowledge in Chinese society was that of a Taoist called Tung Fong Sok who was known to have possessed the secret of longevity. When Emperor Lau Che asked him for the secret, Tung replied with a smile, "I don't have any particular techniques, but one can

purge the dirt from my bones, tendons and muscles, and one can give me new hair and skin.''

During the period of Northern and Southern States, there was a small country at the bottom of the Himalayas ruled by a Buddhist king. After an invasion by India, that country's prince fled to China and settled in Kwong Tung Province in the south.

The prince was very ugly, and he wore copper rings between his nostrils and a pair on his ear lobes. He was tall with a heavy frame, and people did not like him because he did not wash often. He did not have any social contact, and therefore did not learn the language. His name was Prince Dat Mor.

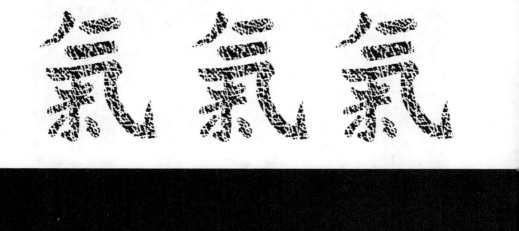

After a time, Prince Dat Mor went north to see the king of the Lang Em-
pire, Siu Hin, to try to convert him to Buddhism. Siu Hin turned him down.
Prince Dat Mor was dejected and left. He crossed the Yantze River to seek a
friendly temple, but was not accepted anywhere. At last he came to Bud Tor
Temple and was admitted there. This temple was renamed during the Tang
Dynasty and is now called the Shaolin Temple. Dat Mor taught the yick kan
ging exercises to the monks there.

The chi exercises described in this book have originated from the exercises
of the yick kan ging taught in the Shaolin Temple, except the prescribed exercises have been perfected by the Shaolin grandmasters through the years.

Contents

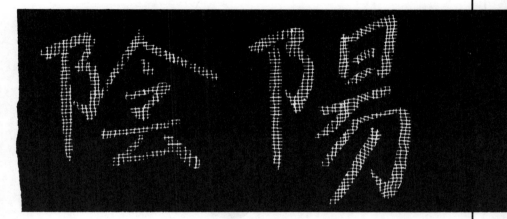

Chapter 1
THE NATURE OF CHI:
YIN / YANG AND THE FIVE ELEMENTS

The *Nei Ching,* or the *Yellow Emperor's Classic of Internal Medicine,* is the earliest known text on *chi* (internal power). It is believed to have been written during the reign of Emperor Huang Ti (2697-2596 B.C.). The *Nei Ching* elaborately outlines a systematic method of therapy:

The root of the way of life, or birth and change is chi; the myriad things of heaven and earth all obey this law. Thus chi in the periphery envelopes heaven and earth; chi in the interior activates them. The source wherefrom the sun, moon, and stars derive their light; the thunder, rain, wind and cloud, their being, the four seasons and the myriad things their birth, growth, gathering and storing; all this is brought about by chi. Man's possession of life is completely dependent upon this chi.

—Nei Ching

The Chinese structured their universe out of ever-changing energies. The balance and harmony of these energies they call "Tao." Tao is not a thing, it is merely a word.

Tao contains the totality of all energy. It exists in the constant state of movement and change out of which all things evolve.

One is expressed as

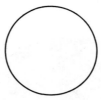

and out of this oneness evolved two, two perfect circles evolving and revolving within the one, the tails of each indicating movement, the eternal revolution.

The dark energy is yin and the bright energy is yang, each holding the seed of each other, and through their continuous evolution, they gave birth to all things, and created their polar opposites.

The Five Elements and Their Cycles of Interaction

The Chinese believe that there are five earthly elements: fire, earth, metal, water, wood. There are two cycles illustrating the interaction between these elements:

• *The cycle of generation*—element generates or produces the succeeding element. Thus fire produces earth, earth produces metal, metal produces water, water produces wood, wood produces fire, fire produces earth.

• *The cycle of destruction*—each element destroys or absorbs the succeeding element. Fire destroys metal, metal destroys wood, wood destroys earth, earth destroys water, water destroys fire.

Interaction of the Five Elements

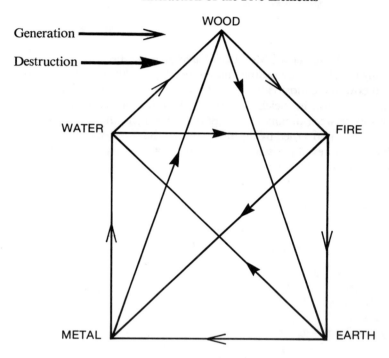

Body Equilibrium

The elements, together with yin and yang, will determine the state of balance and equilibrium within the body. The five elements, as assigned to the organs and bowels, are:

	Wood	*Fire*	*Earth*	*Metal*	*Water*
Yin:	Liver	Heart	Spleen	Lung	Kidney
Yang:	Gall Bladder	Small Intestine	Stomach	Large Intestine	Bladder

Each organ and bowel is governed by two meridians: one flows from the left; one from the right. The pressure points are the breathing points for the meridians. There are eight other extraordinary meridians which provide for energy to continue its cycle of circulation, regardless of whether any one of the organs or bowels becomes decreased and blocks the meridian's circuit. There are other pressure points that cannot be traced to have any connections with the meridians.

Timetable of Meridians Governing Organs

Following is a clock showing the times of the day that the meridians of the organs and bowels are most vulnerable. This is one of the basic principles by which Chinese doctors in ancient days treated illnesses. Furthermore, there is a relationship between organs which are opposite each other on the clock. This relationship is governed by the interaction of the five elements. Treating the gall bladder, for example, which belongs to the wood element, benefits the heart which is of the fire element.

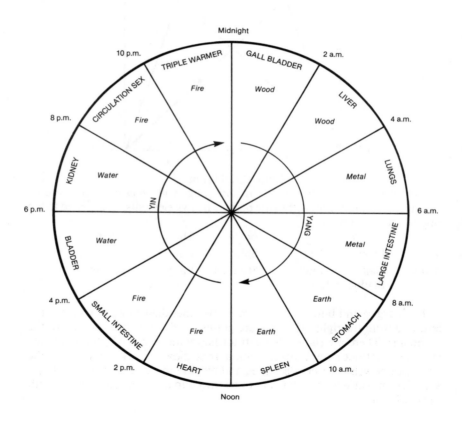

The Death Touch

The death touch, or *dim mak*, is a specialized technique requiring the striking of a particularly vital pressure point at a certain time of the day and season. This deadly art was developed by the highly skilled kung fu practitioners through the centuries, and is based on this relationship between the vital pressure points, the various organs, and chi.

Because the wing chun style was developed by a woman, the emphasis is on the efficiency of the strike, and dim mak is one of its secret specialties. Nevertheless, a lot of the training is devoted to healing the victims of the death touch with the use of different combinations cf herbal formulas and pressure-point massage.

Chapter 2
THE FLOW OF CHI:
PRESSURE POINTS AND MERIDIANS

There are 32 known meridians of which 24 belong to the organs and bowels while the other eight govern other functions of the body. Each organ and bowel has a pair of meridians: one flows on the right side and one flows on the left side.

One can imagine the meridian as a train route. The pressure point is like a train station and the commuters are the *chi* (internal energy) which flows along the meridian. The chi gets on and off at the pressure point as the commuters get on and off at the train stations.

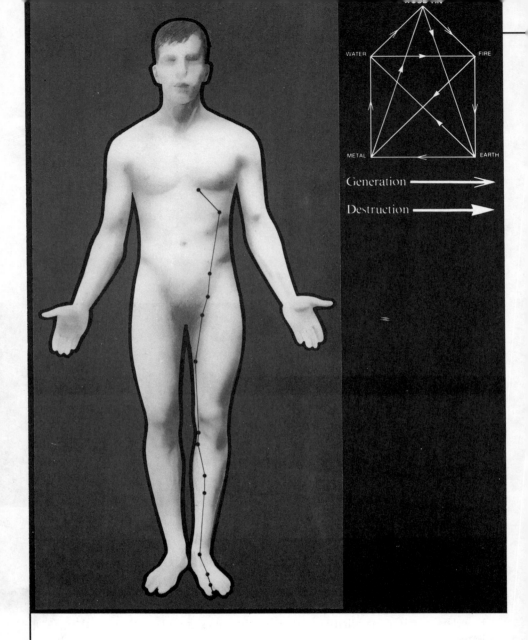

Generation →

Destruction →

Liver Meridians

There are two liver meridians. They belong to the wood element and are yin property. Each liver meridian has 14 pressure points. The liver meridians control the funcitons of sex organs, digestion, urination, chest and the inside of the legs. Of course these meridians also govern the liver.

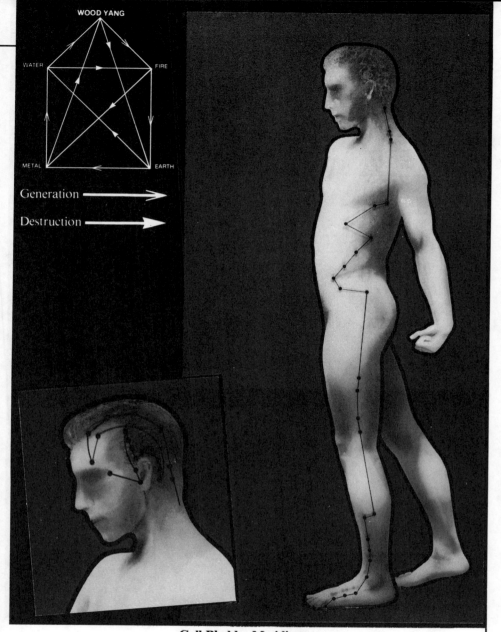

Gall Bladder Meridians

The gall bladder meridians are in charge of the gall bladder. Each has 44 pressure points. Each commences from the corner of the eye running right down from the neck to the chest, down the side of the body, the outside of the leg to the little toe. The gall bladder meridians are responsible for the head, the eye, the ear, the nose, the mouth, the throat, fever, chest, outside leg and lower leg. They are the family of wood, and are yang property.

27

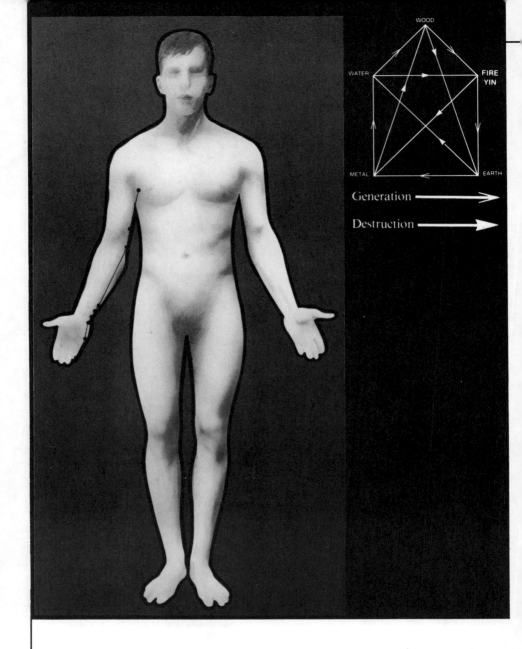

Heart Meridians

The heart meridians each have nine pressure points. They are the element of fire and are yin property. They are a means of controlling heart disease, insomnia and inside arm problems.

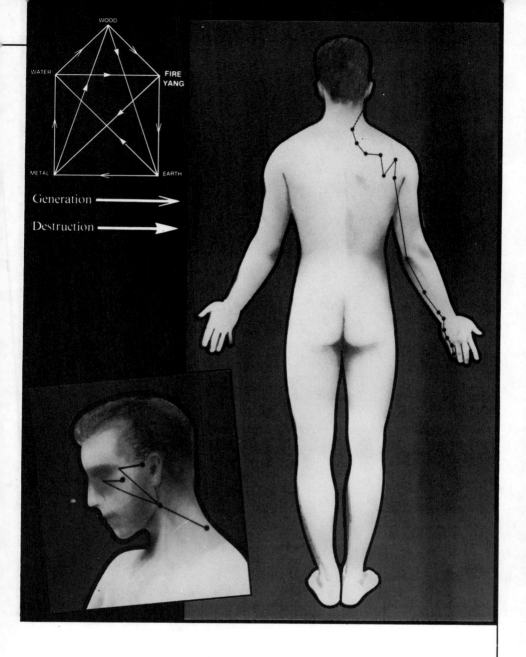

Small Intestine Meridians

The small intestine meridians also belong to the element of fire and are yang property. Each has 19 pressure points. Proper exercise of these pressure points can help problems with eyes, ears, nose, fever, stiff neck and the outside of the arm.

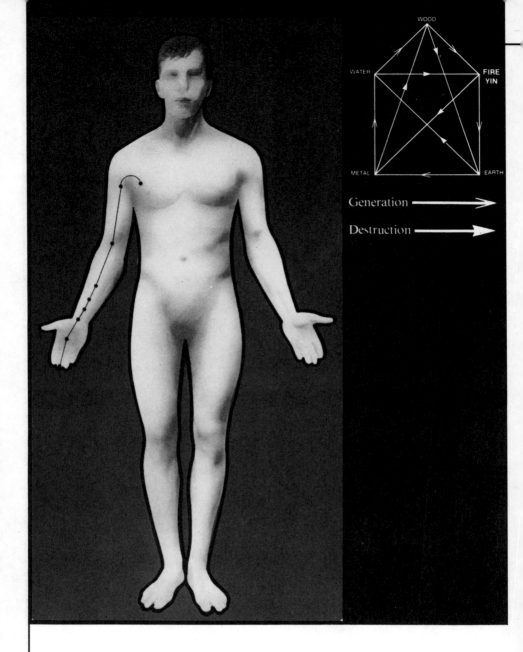

Circulation/Sex Meridians

The circulation/sex meridians also belong to the element of fire, and are yin property. Each meridian has nine pressure points. The proper exercise of these pressure points can cure heart trouble, loss of memory and inside arm problems.

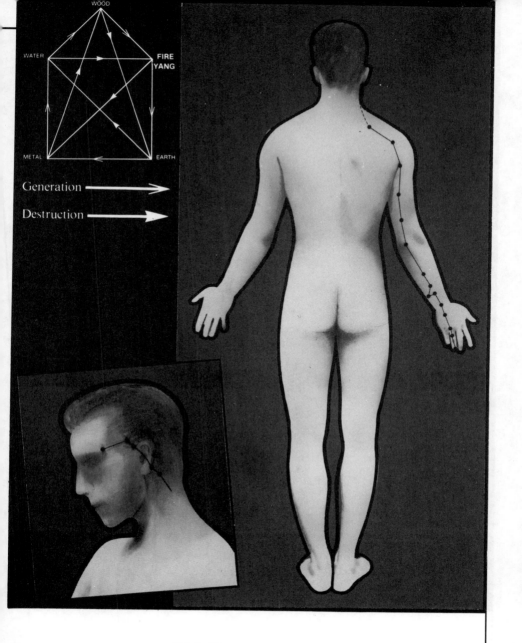

Triple Warmer Meridians

The triple warmer meridians are the element of fire, and are yang property. Each meridian has 23 pressure points. The proper exercise of the pressure points can be used to cure problems of eyes, ears, mouth, nose, throat, fever, chest, lack of energy and outside of the arms.

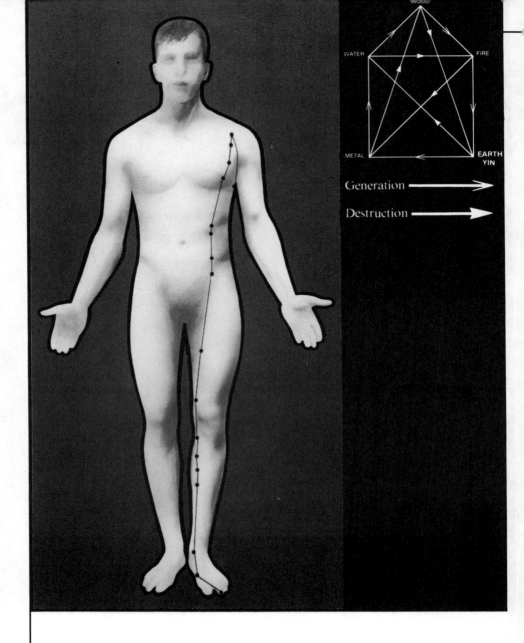

WOOD

WATER

FIRE

METAL

EARTH
YIN

Generation ⟶

Destruction ⟶

Spleen Meridians

The spleen meridians belong to the element of earth and are yin property. Each meridian has 20 pressure points and with proper exercise these pressure points can cure problems of the stomach, urination, sex organ and inside of the leg.

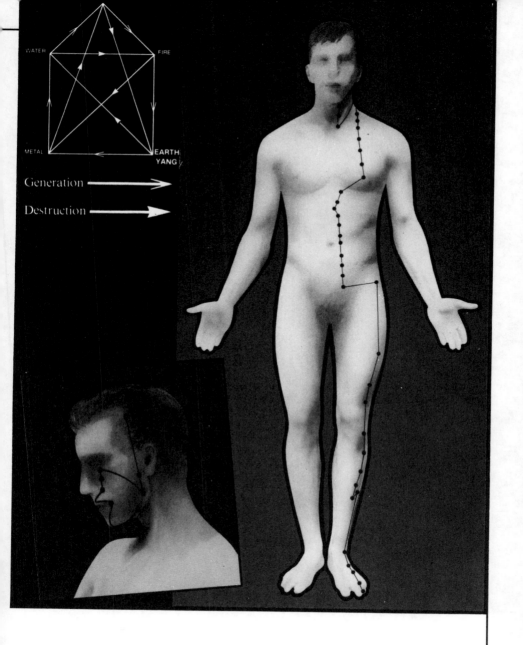

WATER   FIRE

METAL   EARTH, YANG

Generation ⟶

Destruction ⟶

Stomach Meridians

The stomach meridians belong to the element of earth, and are yang property. Each meridian has 45 pressure points, and proper exercise of these meridians can help problems of the stomach, intestine, eyes, nose, mouth, ears, fever, deliriousness, chest and outside legs.

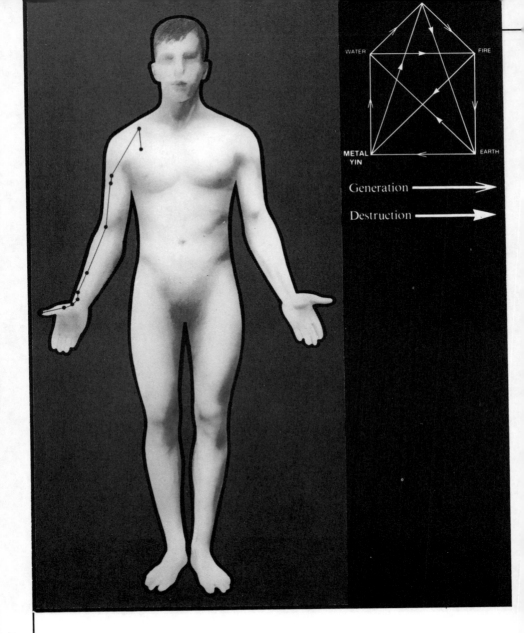

WATER

FIRE

METAL
YIN

EARTH

Generation ⟶

Destruction ⟶

Lung Meridians

The lung meridians belong to the element of metal and are yin property. Each meridian has 11 pressure points and proper exercise of these meridians can help problems with breathing, sore throat and sore arms.

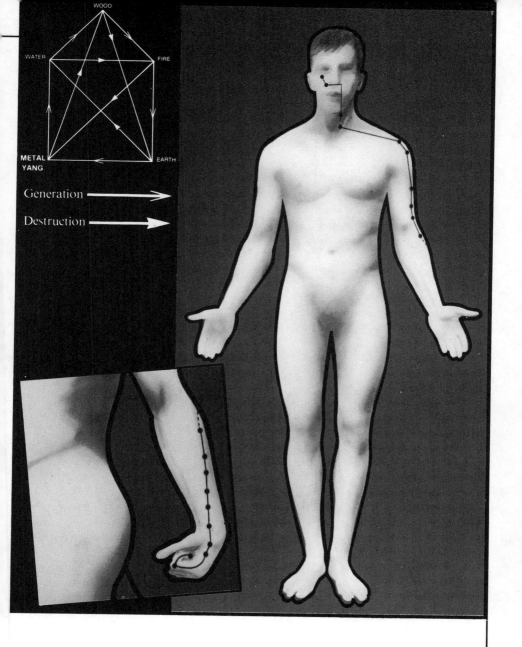

WOOD

WATER   FIRE

METAL
YANG   EARTH

Generation ⟶

Destruction ⟶

Large Intestine Meridians

The large intestine meridians belong to the element of metal, and are yang property. Each meridian has 20 pressure points. Proper exercise of these meridians can help problems of the eyes, throat, nose, mouth, flu and outside arms.

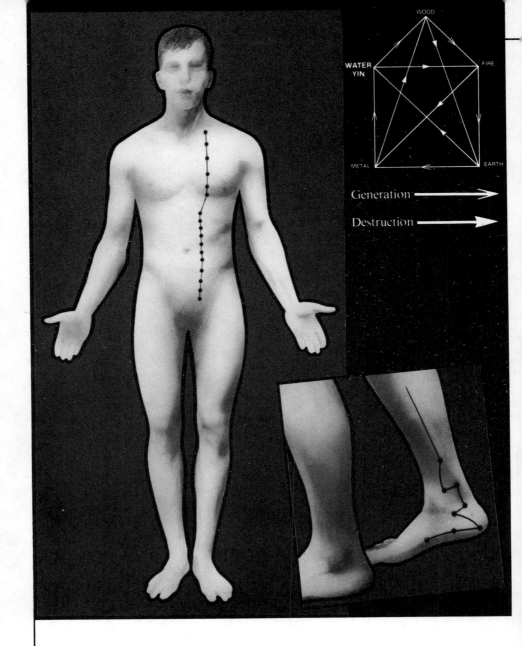

WOOD

WATER
YIN

FIRE

METAL

EARTH

Generation →

Destruction →

Kidney Meridians

The kidney meridians belong to the element of water, and are yin property. Each meridian has 27 pressure points, and proper exercise of these meridians can help the sex organs, urination, lungs, throat and inside of the legs.

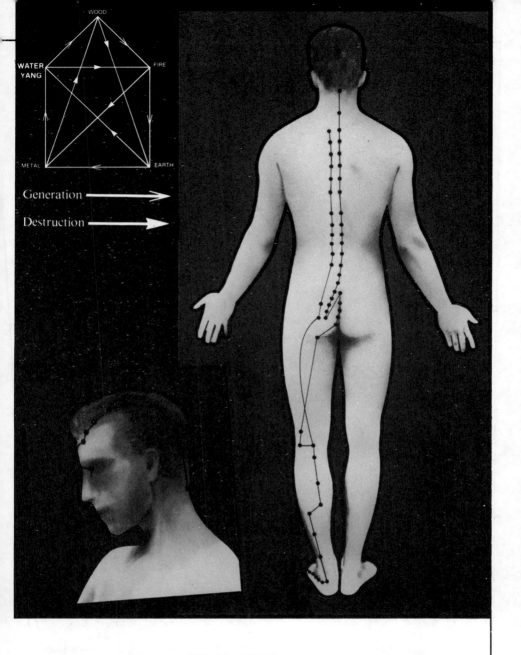

Generation ⟶

Destruction ⟶

Bladder Meridians

The bladder meridians belong to the element of water, and are yang property. Each meridian has 67 pressure points, and proper exercise of these meridians can help problems with the eyes, ears, mouth, throat, shoulder, neck, back, kidney, hips, legs and bladder.

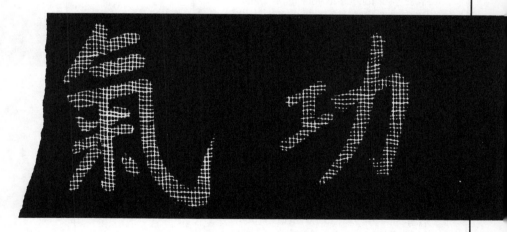

Chapter 3
PROMOTING THE FLOW OF CHI: CHI EXERCISES

The breathing exercises or chi exercises are for the benefit of the back trunk meridian and the front trunk meridian. They are the most fundamental and beneficial group of exercises for those seeking to develop their chi.

Massaging certain major pressure points as a form of exercise has the effect of ensuring the smooth flow of chi throughout the body. In this chapter, these pressure points are delineated, and the best method for massaging each of them is given. These pressure-point exercises will help you to maintain your general health.

Breathing Exercise

(1) Begin by standing with feet shoulder width apart, knees bent slightly, and pushing toward each other. The head and body are in a straight line. The pelvis is pushed forward and the eyes are focused at a far distance. Place both hands one foot in front of your chest, palms facing each other about one-and-a-half inches apart to form a circuit such that the chi will travel from the left palm to the right. Press your tongue to your upper palate. There is a pressure point there. At the same time, this will produce a lot of saliva which you swallow. Breathe out before breathing in to complete one cycle. When we are born, we contain a breath of air and so we commence the breathing exercise by breathing out first. Do not force your breath. Breathe out through your nose and imagine the air coming from the lower abdomen, up through your chest, and out your nose. Inhale through your nose and imagine the air going up into your head, passing down your back and into the lower abdomen to complete one cycle. Do the exercise for nine cycles. (2&3) Keep the palms an inch-and-a-half apart, and roll them to the left of the body, and breathe out at the same time. (4) With the left palm facing up and the right palm facing down, commence the breathing exercise for nine cycles. (5) Begin rolling your palms toward the center position, and as they move together in that direc-

Continued

tion, breathe out. (6) Breathe in as your palms reach the center position. (7) Begin rolling your palms to the right side of your body as you breathe out. (8) Breathe in as your palms reach the right side position. (9) With the right palm facing down over the left which is facing up, breathe for nine cycles. (10) Begin moving your palms together toward the center position, and as they move together in that direction, breathe out. (11) Breathe in as your palms reach the center position to end the exercise.

Close Up

Close Up

Pressure Point Exercises

(1) Massage the pressure point *hoku* of the large intestine meridian on the left hand located between the base of the thumb and the base of the forefinger. Massage this point with your right thumb, and simultaneously breathe nine cycles. Repeat for the right side. (2) Massage the pressure point *chuchih* of the large intestine meridian on the left arm located on the end of the crease of the elbow. Massage it with your right thumb, and simultaneously breathe nine cycles. Repeat

for the right side. (3) Massage pressure point *chutse* of the sex meridian. On the left side, this point is located at the middle of the left inside elbow. Massage it with your right thumb, and simultaneously breathe nine cycles. Repeat for the right side. (4) Massage pressure point *shaohai* of the heart meridian. On the left side, this point is located at the crease of the left inside elbow. Massage it with your right thumb, and simultaneously breathe nine cycles. Repeat for the right

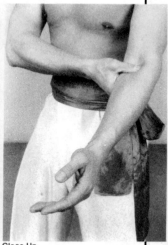

Close Up

Close Up

Continued

5

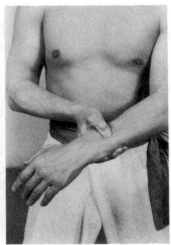

Close Up

6

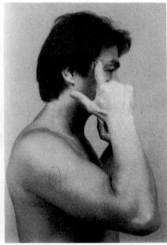

Close Up

side. (5) Massage pressure point *chihkou* of the triple warmer meridian. On the left side, this point is located about one-third the distance from your wrist to your elbow on the outside of the left forearm. Massage it with your right thumb and simultaneously breathe nine cycles. Repeat for the right side. (6) Massage pressure point *suchukung* of the triple warmer meridian at the end of the eyebrow close to the right temple with the right index finger. Simultaneously breathe nine cycles. Repeat for the left side. (7) Massage pressure point

7

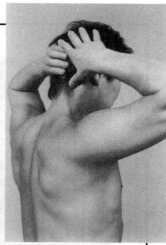

Close Up

chienching of the gall bladder meridian at the top of the right shoulder with the left middle finger. Simultaneously breathe nine cycles. Repeat for the left side. (8) Massage pressure point *chienyu* of the large intestine meridian at the corner of the right shoulder with the middle and index fingers. Simultaneously breathe nine cycles. Repeat for the left side. (9) Massage pressure point *chihchien* of the gall bladder meridian at the base of the skull on the right side. Simultaneously breathe nine cycles. Repeat for the left side.

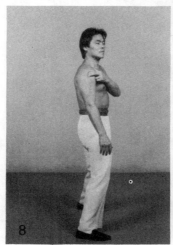

8

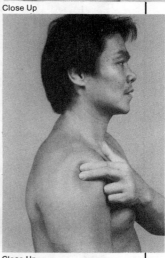

Close Up

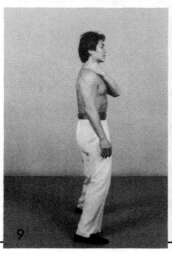

9

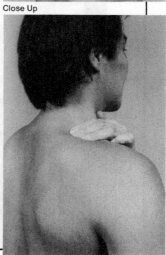

Close Up

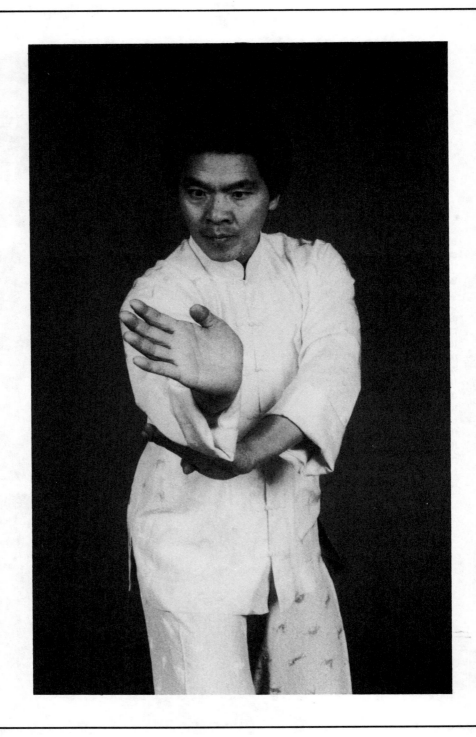

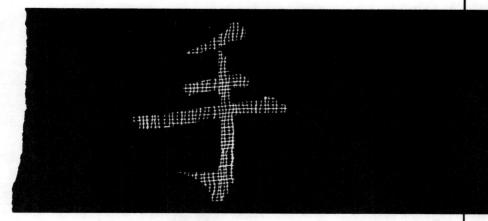

Chapter 4
TECHNIQUES: BASIC ARM MOVEMENTS

The movements of the Shil Lim Tao Form are based on the techniques used in the art of wing chun kung fu. This chapter gives a detailed description of each of the movements as they are used in the form.

They are also used in the two man exercises in which you engage the chi of another person. These movements therefore are the basics which are necessary for the further cultivation of chi and the ability to apply this internal energy in an external physical way.

In this and the following chapter the flow of chi is indicated by directional arrows. These arrows should not be understood to indicate the movement of the body but only the direction in which the chi flows in performing the movements. Sometimes the direction of the chi is the same as the direction of movement, but sometimes it is not, and can even run counter to it. Three types of chi flow are described here, indicated by three corresponding types of arrows.

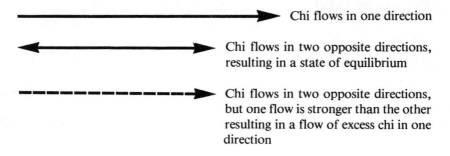

Chi flows in one direction

Chi flows in two opposite directions, resulting in a state of equilibrium

Chi flows in two opposite directions, but one flow is stronger than the other resulting in a flow of excess chi in one direction

Noy Moon Chuie
(Vertical Punch)

The contact areas used for the vertical punch are the knuckles of the little, ring, and middle fingers. The knuckle of the index finger is not used. (1) With your fist tucked in close to your chest on the centerline of your body, (2&3) drive the punch directly forward, keeping your fist in close alignment with the centerline of your body, and making sure to strike with the lower three knuckles.

2

3

Wung Jeung
(Sideward Palm Strike)

(1) With palm facing forward, fingertips angled outward, and elbow close to the centerline of the body, (2) drive your hand forward forcefully, keeping it in the center. The contact area of this strike is the palm of the hand.

Dai Jeung
(Downward Palm Strike)

For dai jeung, (1) your hand should be opened, palm forward with fingers pointing down, and elbow tucked in close alignment with your centerline. (2) Drive your palm directly forward, maintaining your hand in the palm forward position, fingers pointing down. The contact area is the palm of the hand.

Huen Sao
(Circling Wrist Block)

Huen sao done with the left hand, involves a clockwise rotation of the wrist while huen sao done with the right hand involves a counterclockwise rotation. (1) With your hand extended in the palm up position, (2) flex your wrist to point your fingertips toward you as you rotate your hand. (3&4) Continue the rotation downward and (5) outward so your fingertips are pointing to the outside as you (6) begin to bring them up. (7&8) Complete the rotation by bringing your hand into an upright position aligned vertically with the centerline of your body.

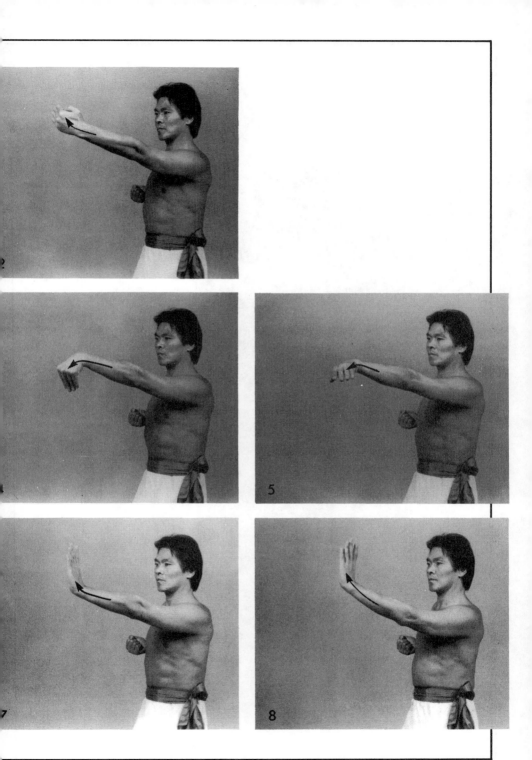

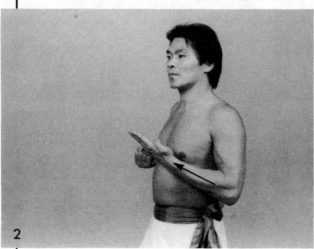

Tan Sao
(Palm Up Block)

(1) Open your hand palm up, keeping your fingers tightly together. (2) Extend your hand in the palm up position. (3) Drive it forward and

up to (4) face level, inclined palm up about 45 degrees. Keep your elbow in close alignment with the center-line of your body.

3

4

Wu Sao
(Vertical Palm Block)

(1) With your hand extended, held upright and aligned vertically with the centerline of your body, (2) draw your hand back toward your face, maintaining the upright position. (3) Pull your hand back to a position about six inches in front of your face.

2

3

59

Fook Sao
(Hook Hand Block)

In fook sao, your wrist is bent so that your fingertips are pointing back toward you. (1) With your hand in this position in front of your chest, (2-4) extend it forward, keeping your elbow in close alignment with the centerline of your body. Extend it directly forward at chest level.

Pak Sao
(Slap Block)

To execute pak sao, (1) place your hand in an upright open position, fingers together. Begin with your hand close to your body but off to the side. (2) Then, bring your hand across your body to the opposite side, maintaining the upright position of the hand as it moves from one side to the other.

Forward Gum Sao
(Push Block)

Gum sao is fundamentally a push, and it can be done in a forward or backward direction. To perform the forward gum sao, (1) begin with both hands open close to your body, palms facing foward. (2) Push both palms directly forward until (3) both arms are fully extended. Be sure to maintain the palm-forward position of both hands.

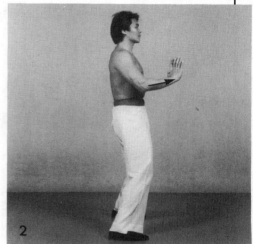

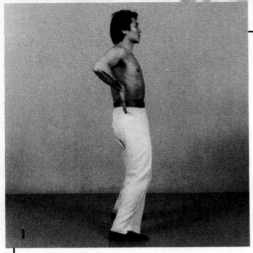

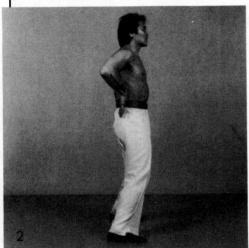

Backward Gum Sao
(Push Block)

To execute backward gum sao, (1) begin with both hands in an open position, aligned vertically at either side of your body at waist level, palms facing backward. Your elbows are flexed. (2&3) Push backward and down with both palms until both arms are fully extended. As you push, your wrists flex back so that your fingertips point forward, exposing your palms obliquely downward.

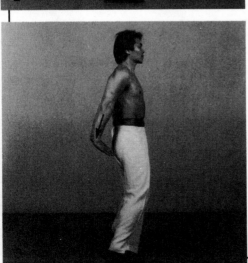

Fut Sao
(Outward Down Block)

(1) Place both hands in the open position, palms facing inward just in front of your hips. Your elbows are flexed. (2) Spread both hands out to the sides maintaining the backward facing direction of the palms. (3) As both arms swing upward into a fully extended position, the palms rotate to a downward facing direction.

Jut Sao
(Jerking Hand Block)

(1) Begin with your forearms and open hands aligned vertically in front of your body, palms inward, and elbows tucked. (2) Drive your hands forward, keeping your elbows as close as possible to the centerline, to a position with palms facing obliquely upward. (3) Then rotate both arms quickly so that your elbows swing outward, and both palms turn obliquely downward, dropping from face level to chest level.

1

Bil Sao
(Finger Thrust Block)

(1) With both hands about a foot in front of
your body, palms facing obliquely downward at chin level, elbows angled outward
slightly, (2) drive both hands fingertips forward until both arms are fully extended
with both hands curved slightly inward.

2

Bon Sao
(Raised Elbow Block)

To execute bon sao, (1) open your hand in the palm up position, and as you (2) extend it forward and up, rotate your entire arm so that (3) your elbow is turned up, raised to brow level, and your forearm angles downward, and your palm is turned to face to the outside.

1

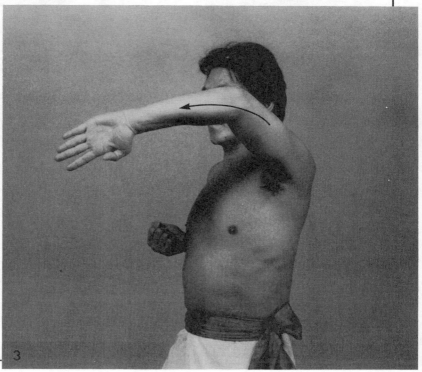

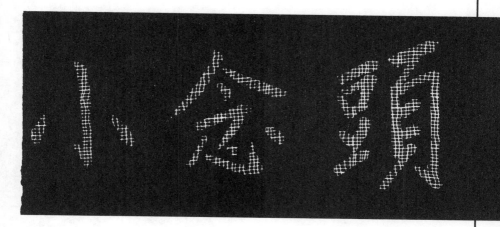

Chapter 5
CULTIVATING CHI:
THE SHIL LIM TAO FORM

This is the first form in wing chun kung fu. It is designed to train for improvement of breathing, coordination, concentration, balance, independent movement of the limbs, and mind and body coordination. Most important of all, doing this form improves the internal energy flow.

This form is divided into four sections:

1. Commencement;
2. Tan sao and fook sao;
3. Gum sao and bil sao; and
4. Tan sao, garn sao, and bon sao

Throughout this form you should maintain full concentration. Look straight ahead, and touch your tongue to your upper palate of your mouth. With mouth closed, breathe normally through your nose. Whenever you use your palm, keep your fingers together and your thumb tucked in tightly so that your fingers and thumb are protected. Similarly, when using a fist, curl the fingers tightly, and place the thumb over the second section of the index finger.

In the neutral stance, keep your feet slightly wider apart than shoulder width with both feet parallel to each other. Squat down slightly, squeeze the knees toward each other, and push your tail forward. Your head, neck, and body should be aligned, and your thigh and buttocks should be tensed so that the energy can travel to the upper part of the body, generated from the thigh muscle, the largest muscle of the body.

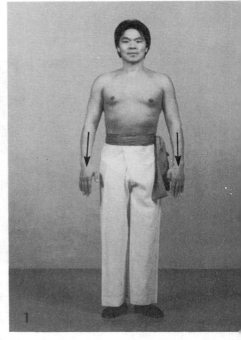

Commencement

(1) From the ready position with your tongue touching your upper palate, train your eyes at a far distance, concentrate, and breathe normally. (2) Raise both arms up to shoulder level, and (3) clench them into fists. (4) Turn your fists palm side upward, and (5&6) pull them toward your body, keeping them as high as possible without touching your body. This opens

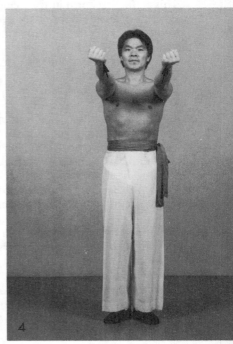

3

6

Continued

7

up the lungs. (7) Flex your knees, squatting down slightly to lower your center of gravity and improve your stability. (8&9) Swing your left foot in an arc out to the left side to a distance just wider than shoulder width. (10) Bring your right foot in next to your left. (11&12) Swing your right foot out in the same manner to the

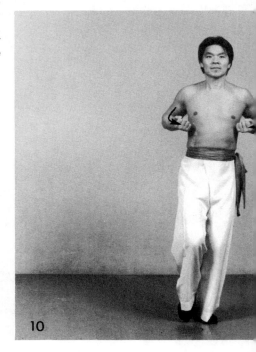

10

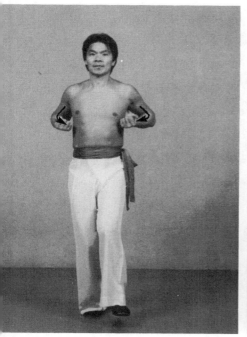

9

1

12

Continued

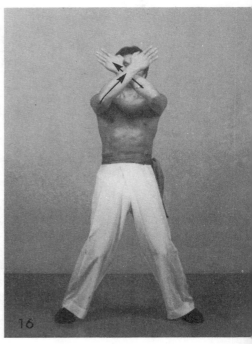

right side to form a neutral stance. (13) Open your hands and position them in front of your chest. (14) Extend your arms forward and down, crossing them left over right. (15) Fold your arms in front of your chest with the right arm on the outside. (16) Clench your hands into fists, and (17) bring your fists back to their original positions beside your body. (18) Bring your left fist in front of your chest,

14

15

17

18

Continued

19

and (19&20) push your left fist forward. Exhale as you execute this slow vertical punch. (21) Open your palm facing upward, and (22-24) execute huen sao, rotat-

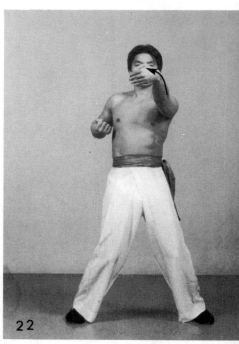

22

20

21

23

24

Continued

ing the wrist clockwise. (25) Clench your left hand into a fist, and (26&27) bring your fist back to your body. (28) Bring your right fist in front of your chest and (29&30) exhale as you execute a slow vertical punch. (31) Open your right palm facing upward.

25

28

29

27

31

Continued

(32-35) Execute huen sao, rotating the wrist counterclockwise. (36) Clench your right hand into a fist, and (37&38) pull it back toward your body.

32

35

36

33

34

37

38

85

Tan Sao and Fook Sao

(1) Open your left palm and drive it forward from the center of the body, executing a tan sao. (2) Keep your elbow close to the centerline of the body as you execute the tan sao, and stop the motion when the elbow reaches a distance of about five inches from the chest. (3-6) Execute huen sao, rotating the wrist clockwise, and stopping at the wu sao position. Make sure your elbow is placed slightly outside the

2

3

5

6

Continued

body. (7&8) Bring your hand in the wu sao position in toward the body along the centerline, keeping your elbow slightly outside the body. (9) Change to fook sao by bending the wrist and making sure that the hand is diagonally placed. (10&11) Drive fook sao out horizontally along the centerline and keep your elbow close to the centerline. Stop the action when the elbow reaches five inches from the chest. (12-14) Execute huen sao, rotating the

7

10

8

9

11

12

Continued

wrist clockwise, stopping at the wu sao position, and making sure that the elbow is placed slightly outside the body. (15-17) Bring wu sao in toward the body along the centerline, keeping your elbow slightly outside the body. (18) Change to fook sao by bending the wrist and making sure that

13

16

14

15

17

18

Continued

the hand is diagonally placed. (19&20) Drive fook sao out horizontally along the centerline and keep your elbow close to the centerline. Stop the action when the elbow reaches five inches from the chest. (21-23) Execute huen sao, rotating the wrist clockwise, stopping at the wu sao position, and making sure that the elbow is placed outside the body. (24-27) Bring

19

22

20

21

23

24

Continued

wu sao in toward the body along the centerline, keeping the elbow slightly outside the body. (28) Change to fook sao by bending the wrist and making sure that the hand is diagonally placed. (29&30) Drive fook sao out horizontally along the centerline and keep your elbow close to the centerline. Stop the action when the elbow reaches five inches from the chest.

25

28

26

27

29

30

Continued

31

(31-33) Execute huen sao, rotating the wrist clockwise, stopping at the wu sao position, and making sure that the elbow is placed outside the body. (34-37) Bring wu sao in toward the body along the centerline, keeping the elbow slightly outside

34

32

33

35

36

Continued

the body. (38) Execute pak sao. Push diagonally upward and across the body. (39) Position your palm in front of your chest, keeping the elbow close to the centerline, ready for a vertical palm strike. (40) Exhale as you execute wung jeung. (41) Turn your palm upward, and (42-46) execute huen

38

39

1

42

Continued

43

sao, rotating the wrist clockwise. (47) Clench your hand into a fist, and (48) pull it back to the side of your body in the neutral stance. Repeat steps 1 through 48 for the right side.

46

44

45

47

48

Gum Sao and Bil Sao

(1&2) Exhale as you execute a left gum sao. Push your palm down and away from your body to the left side, making sure the wrist is locked and the contact area is the side of the palm. (3-5) Keeping your left hand in the gum sao position, exhale as

5

Continued

you execute a right gum sao. (6) Pull your elbows up and place your palms behind your back in preparation for a backward gum sao. (7) Execute a backward gum sao, striking with the side of the palms. Exhale while executing this. (8) Pull your elbows up and position your palms in front of your chest in preparation for a forward gum sao. (9) Execute a forward gum sao, pushing both palms down and out away from the body. Exhale as you do this, and make sure the contact area is the side of the palm. (10) Fold your arms in front of your chest without having them touch with the left arm over the right. (11) Drop the elbows, preparing for fut sao.

8

11

Continued

(12-14) Execute fut sao, swinging the arms outward. Exhale as you perform this. (15&16) Fold your arms in front of your chest with the right arm over the left. (17&18) Execute a double tan sao by un-

12

15

13

14

5

17

Continued

folding your arms upward, then immediately (19) execute a double jut sao by suddenly turning your arms inward and pulling them in toward the body. (20&21) Execute a double bil sao, sharply thrusting the fingers out with the arm, pivoting both wrists outward. Exhale while executing this. (22&23) Execute a double gum sao

18

21

9

20

2

23

Continued

along the centerline. (24&25) Execute a double tarn sao, pulling both arms up while bending the wrists, with the intention of bouncing off an oncoming attack. (26) Turn both palms upward, preparing for double huen sao. (27-31) Execute a

24

27

25

26

28

29

Continued

double huen sao, rotating the left arm clockwise and the right arm counterclockwise simultaneously. (32) Clench both hands into fists. (33-35) Assume the neutral stance by pulling both fists alongside the body.

30

33

1

32

4

35

Tan Sao, Garn Sao, and Bon Sao

(1&2) Execute pak sao with the left hand. (3) Position your left palm at the center of your body, keeping your elbow close to the centerline in preparation for wung jeung. (4) Execute wung jeung as you exhale. (5) Turn your palm facing upward. (6-8) Execute huen sao, rotating your wrist

Continued

7

clockwise. (9) Clench your hand into a fist, and (10&11) pull it back alongside your body into the neutral stance. (12-14) Exe-

10

8

9

11

12

Continued

cute a right pak sao, pushing across your body from right to left. (15&16) Execute a right wung jeung as you exhale. (17) Turn your palm facing upward. (18-21) Execute

14

15

7

18

Continued

19

huen sao with the left hand, turning your wrist counterclockwise and (22) clench it into a fist. (23&24) Pull it back alongside

22

20

21

23

24

Continued

25

your body into the neutral stance. (25-28) Execute tan sao by scooping the left arm from underneath upward with the elbow ending up along the centerline of the body. (29-32) Execute garn sao, swinging

28

26

27

9

30

Continued

your arm from underneath, close to the centerline. (33&34) Execute tan sao, bringing the arm over from the inside to the palm-up blocking position. (35-37) Exe-

33

36

Continued

37

cute huen sao, rotating the wrist clock-
wise, and prepare for a wung jeung. (38)
Exhale as you execute wung jeung. (39-43)
Execute huen sao, rotating the wrist

40

38

39

42

Continued

43

clockwise, and (44) clench your hand into a fist, and (45&46) pull it back alongside your body into the neutral stance. (47-51) Execute tan sao, sweeping the arm from

46

45

48

Continued

129

49

underneath up along the centerline so that the elbow ends up on the centerline. (52-54) Execute garn sao, swinging your arm from underneath, close to the center-

52

50

51

3

54

Continued

55

line. (55-57) Swing your arm over and back to the tan sao position. (58-61) Execute huen sao, rotating the wrist counterclock-

58

56

57

59

60

Continued

61

wise, and prepare for a wung jeung. (62) Execute wung jeung to the neck. (63) Turn your hand palm upward, and (64-67) exe-

64

62

63

65

66

Continued

67

cute huen sao, rotating the wrist counter-clockwise. (68) Clench your hand into a fist, and (69&70) pull it back alongside your body into the neutral stance. (71-73) With your left arm, execute bon sao, lift-

70

68

69

71

72

Continued

73

ing your elbow and your forearm in front of your body. (74) Drop your fingers down. (75) Execute dai jeung, thrusting from underneath upward. Exhale while performing this. (76) Turn your hand palm upward, and (77-80) execute huen sao, rotating

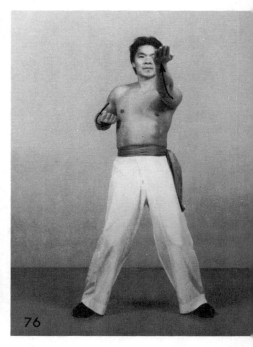

76

74

75

77

78

Continued

79

your wrist clockwise. (81) Clench your hand into a fist, and (82&83) pull your fist back alongside your body into the neutral stance. (84-86) With your right arm, exe-

82

80

81

83

84

Continued

85

cute bon sao, lifting your elbow and your forearm in front of your body. (87&88) Execute tan sao, and (89) drop your fingers down. (90) Execute dai jeung as you ex-

88

86

87

89

90

Continued

91

hale. (91) Turn your hand palm upward, and (92-96) execute huen sao, rotating the

94

92

93

95

96

Continued

wrist counterclockwise. (97) Clench your hand into a fist, and (98-100) pull it back alongside your body into the neutral stance. (101) Bring your left foot next to your right, and (102-103) return to an upright position.

98

99

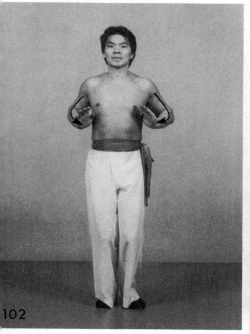

102

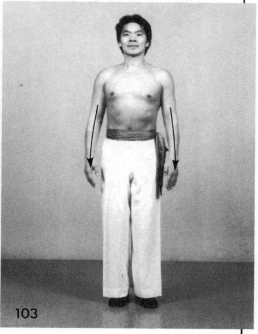

103

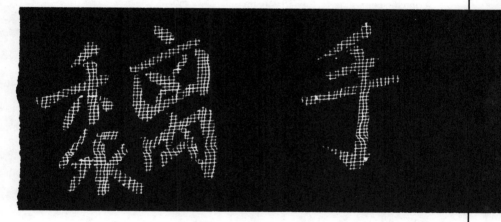

Chapter 6
ENGAGING AN OPPONENT'S CHI:
BASIC CHI SAO EXERCISES

Chi sao is for the training of coordination, balance, reflexes, and close-range vision. More importantly, chi sao develops internal energy and the ability to strike at close range.

We all know that force has only one direction, but the force developed in chi sao can be interpreted as a force with several directions, like a guided missile following its target. This force can only be acquired from proper wing chun chi sao exercises.

Fook Sao Drill

(1) From the neutral stance with your left arm tucked next to your body, extend your right arm in a fook sao position. (2&3) Execute jut sao, pushing your wrist down along the centerline. (4) Clench your hand into a fist in preparation for a vertical punch. (5) Execute the vertical punch, and (6&7) return your right hand to the fook sao position.

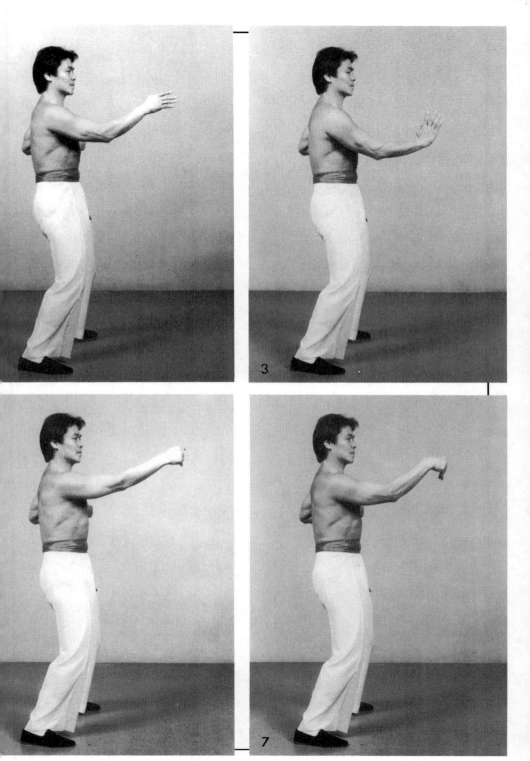

3

7

151

Tan Sao Drill

(1) From a neutral stance with the left arm tucked alongside the body, extend your right arm in the tan sao position. (2&3) Execute a vertical palm strike, and (4&5) follow immediately with a bon sao. (6&7) Return your hand to the tan sao position.

3

7

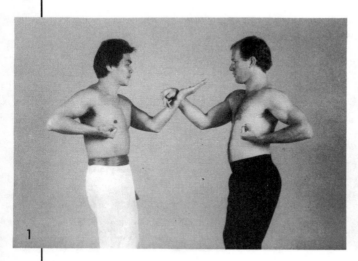

Application of the One-Arm Drills

The previous two drills complement each other in this two-man exercise. The positions should also be reversed, but here (1) you assume the tan sao position and your partner uses the fook sao position. (2) As you execute the palm strike, your

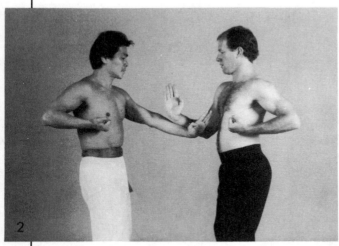

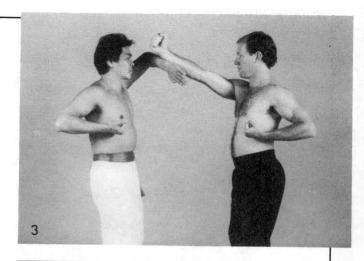

3

partner blocks with jut sao. (3) Your partner executes the vertical punch, and you use bon sao to deflect it. Then (4&5) both return to your respective starting positions. Repeat the exercise by switching your starting positions.

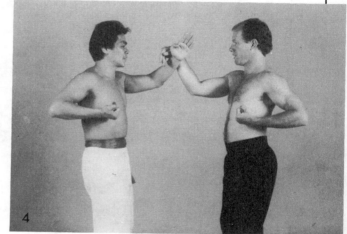

4

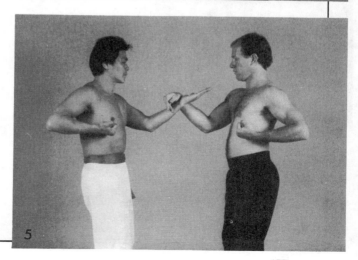

5

Side View

Side View

Two-Arm Drill

(1) With your left arm in fook sao, place your right arm in tan sao, feet in the neutral stance. (2&3) With your left

3

arm remaining in fook sao, execute a vertical palm strike with your right arm. (4&5) With your left arm re-

4

Continued

5

Side View

maining in fook sao, return your right arm to the tan sao position. (6&7) With your left arm remaining in fook sao,

6

Side View

158

Side View

7

execute bon sao with your right arm. (8&9) Execute jut sao with your left arm with your right arm remaining in

Side View

8

Side View

9

Continued

Side View

Side View

bon sao. (10&11) Execute a vertical punch with your left arm with your right arm remaining in bon sao. (12-14) Return your left arm to the

fook sao position, and return your right arm to the tan sao position. Repeat the exercise.

Application of the Two-Arm Drill

The two-arm drill ends when you come back to your starting position, ready to begin again. It forms a cycle. When put in application with a partner, each of you begins in a different step in the cycle so your moves complement each other. (1) You begin with left fook sao and right tan sao. This is step one in the drill. Your partner begins in left fook sao and right bon sao. This is step six of the drill. (2) You execute the vertical palm strike with your right arm, and your partner deflects it by executing the jut sao with his left arm. (3) Your partner executes the vertical punch with his left arm, and you deflect it by returning your right arm to the tan sao position. (4) Your partner returns his left arm to the fook sao position. (5&6) You place your right arm in the bon sao position as your partner places his right arm in the tan sao position. You are now at the step in which your partner started and vice versa. (7) Your partner executes the vertical palm strike with his right arm, and you deflect it by executing the jut sao with your left arm. (8) You execute the vertical punch with your left arm, and your partner deflects it by returning his right arm to the tan sao position. (9) You return your left arm to the fook sao position. To get back to the start, your partner places his right arm in the bon sao position, and you place your right arm in the tan sao position. Then repeat the routine.

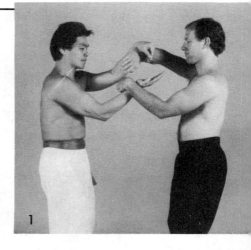

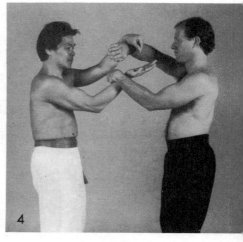

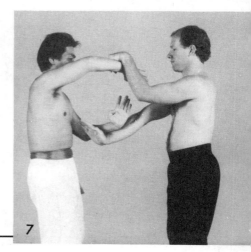

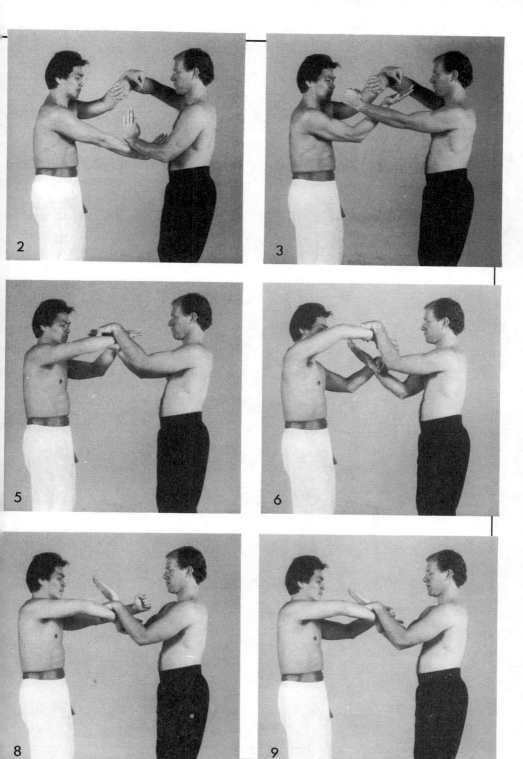

Jut Sao and Garn Sao

(1) With your right arm in bon sao and your left arm in fook sao, you lock up with your partner whose right arm is in tan sao and whose left arm is in fook sao. (2) Your partner strikes with his right palm and you deflect it with a left jut sao. (3) You catch

your partner's right arm with a right garn sao from underneath, and simultaneously strike to the head with your left. (4) Then, trap his right arm with a left pak sao, and punch to the head again with your right fist.

3

4

Larp Sao: One

(1) With your right arm in bon sao, and your left in fook sao, you lock up with your partner who has his right arm in tan sao and his left arm in fook sao. (2) Rotate your right bon sao into tan sao as your partner simultaneously rotates his right tan

sao into bon sao. (3) Change your right tan sao into larp sao, catching your partner's right elbow. (4) Trap your partner's arms with your right larp sao and execute a punch with your left fist to your partner's head.

3

4

Larp Sao: Two

(1) Start with your right arm in tan sao and your left in fook sao. Your partner begins with right bon sao and left fook sao. (2) Simultaneously rotate your right tan sao into bon sao and your left bon sao into tan sao. (3) Release your left fook sao

and execute a left larp sao on your partner's left elbow. (4) Trap your partner's arms with the left larp sao and simultaneously punch to the ribs with your right fist. (5) Then, execute another punch to the head with your right fist.

Larp Sao and Front Kick

(1) With your right arm in bon sao and your left in fook sao, lock up with your partner. His right arm is in tan sao and his left in fook sao. (2) Rotate your right bon sao into tan sao as your partner simultaneously rotates his right tan sao into bon sao.

3

(3) Release your right tan sao and change it into larp sao, trapping your partner's right elbow. (4) Execute a kick to the midsection with your right foot. (5) Move forward, trapping your partner's right elbow, and punch with your left fist to the head.

4

5

Pak Sao

(1) Both you and your partner assume a right front stance facing each other, and cross your right arms. The backs of your wrists pressing together, (2) execute a left pak sao to your partner's right elbow, and (3) follow up with a right punch to his face.

1

2

3

Pak Sao and Garn Sao

(1) Both you and your partner assume a right front stance. Cross your right arms, pressing the backs of your wrists together. (2) Use a left pak sao to block your partner's right elbow, and (3) follow up with a punch to the face. Your partner uses a left pak sao to deflect the punch. (4) Swing your right arm with a garn sao, trap-

174

ping your partner's arms from underneath his right elbow. (5) Execute a left punch to the ribs while maintaining the trap on his right elbow with your right arm. (6) Execute a punch to the head with your left fist still maintaining the trap on your partner's right elbow with your right arm.

Counter Pak Sao and Punch

(1) Both you and your partner assume a front stance with your right arms crossed at the wrists, the backs of your wrists pressing together. (2) Your partner applies a left pak sao to your right elbow to push open your de-

fense. (3) He pushes with his right fist. Execute a left larp sao to deflect the punch. (4) Pull back your right arm and bring it around to punch to your partner's head. (5) Follow up with a left to the head.

Larp Sao

(1) Your partner punches with his left fist and you deflect it with a right bon sao. (2) You use a left larp sao on your partner's left arm. (3) Execute a punch with your right fist, and your partner uses a left bon sao

to deflect it. (4) You use a left larp sao on your partner's right wrist. (5) Your partner punches with his left fist and you deflect it with a left bon sao. Repeat the exercise.

Larp Sao and Punch

(1) Both you and your partner assume a right front stance, the backs of your right wrists crossed and pressing against each other. (2) Execute a right larp

sao to your partner's elbow, turning his body to the right side, and then (3) follow up with a left punch to the ribs, and a (4) left punch to the face.

Counter Larp Sao and Punch

(1) Both you and your part-ner assume a right front stance, the backs of your right wrists crossed and pressing together. (2) Your partner moves in with a right larp sao to your right arm and a left punch for your

head. Use a left garn sao to deflect the punch. (3) Swing your right arm around to execute a larp sao, trapping your partner's right elbow. (4) While maintaining the trap on his right elbow, execute a left punch to the ribs.

Larp Sao and Front Kick

(1) Both you and your partner are in a right front stance with your right arms crossed at the wrists. The backs of your wrists press together. (2) Execute a right larp sao to your partner's

184

right wrist. (3) Execute a right kick to his midsection, then (4) step forward and punch to the head, still maintaining control of his right wrist with your right larp sao.

1

2

Counter Larp Sao and Front Kick

(1) Both you and your partner assume a front stance with the backs of your right wrists crossed. (2) Your partner uses a right larp sao on your right arm, and then (3) follows with a right kick. Step back with your right

foot and use a left gum sao to deflect the kick. (4) Your partner moves up with a left punch to the head, you deflect it with a right larp sao and simultaneously execute a left punch to the face.

3

4

Tsuen Sao

(1) From the ready position, (2) your partner punches with his right fist. You deflect it with a left pak sao. (3) Your partner punches with his left fist and you use a right pak sao to deflect it. (4) Your partner punches with his right fist, and you use a left pak sao to deflect it at the same time that you place your right hand under your own left arm (5) to find your partner's right elbow. (6) Trap your partner's right elbow, and execute a punch to his head with your left fist. (7) While maintaining the trap on his right elbow, follow up with a punch to his ribs.

1

4

5

Inside Pak Sao and Tsuen Sao

(1) Both you and your partner assume a neutral stance. (2) Your partner punches with his left fist, and you deflect it with a left pak sao. (3) Your partner punches with his right fist and you deflect it with a right pak sao from the outside. (4) Your partner punches with his left fist, and you deflect it with a left pak sao, and simultaneously position your right arm underneath his left arm. (5) Use tsuen sao to trap your partner's left elbow, then (6) move up to execute a punch to the head with your left fist.

3

6

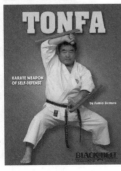

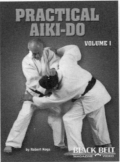